Once upon a time

in

MNYAMA KINGDOM

"Mama I want to be just like papa when I grow up," said Simba the prince as he walks into the bush.
"You will make a very brave king my love" replied Mama.
🐾 🐾 🐾 🐾

"Furaha ♫ Furaha ♫ Furaha ♫ Simba sings happily as he walks in between the trees.

🐾 🐾 🐾 🐾

ROAR!!! Papa roars on top of the mountain.

RAAL!!! Simba tries to roar like Papa.

🐾 🐾 🐾 🐾

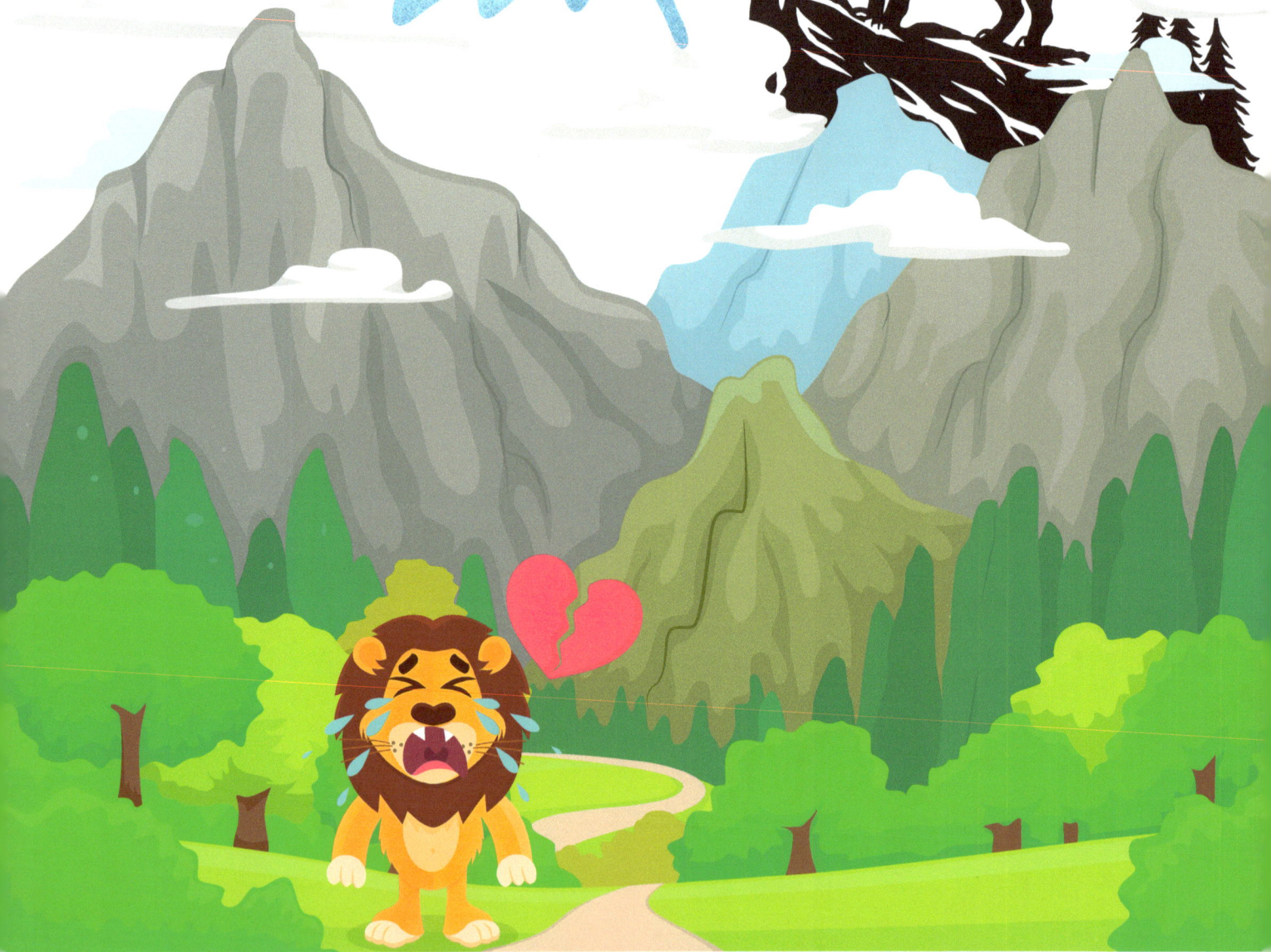

"Oh no!!! My roar is little, I can not roar like Papa" Simba realized and starts to cry.

🐾 🐾 🐾 🐾

"Hello, Simba!!! why do you cry? asked Twiga the giraffe.

"My roar is little, can you teach me, how to roar like my papa?" asks Simba.

"Oh No! giraffes do not roar, go to Kobe the tortoise, he just might be able to teach you" replied Twiga.
🐾 🐾 🐾 🐾

"Hi, Kobe!!! Can you please teach me how to roar like my Papa? Simba desperately asks.

"No my dear Simba, Kobe only makes a wheezing noise, Kobe does not roar," replied Kobe the tortoise.
🐾 🐾 🐾 🐾

Hello

"How do you do, Nyoka!!! do you know how to roar like my Papa? Simba politely asks.

"Never my dear, I'm a snake, and all I do is hiss, not roar," replied Nyoka.
🐾 🐾 🐾 🐾

Hello

"Hey Simba, what are you up to?" asked Tembo the elephant.

"Hello Tembo, I want to learn how to roar like my Papa, can you roar like my papa? asked Simba.

No darling, my loud trumpet sound is no match to your Papa's loud roar. relied Tembo.

"Hello Simba, come play with us,"
says Tumbili the monkey.

"No, I don't want to play, I want
to learn how to roar like my
Papa, can you teach me? asked
Simba.

sorry, Simba monkeys don't roar,
I can only gibber or whoop.
replied Tumbili.

"Hi Simba, do you want to rest under the sun with me?" says Chura the frog.

"I will rest under the sun with you if you teach me how to roar like my papa" replied Simba

No way, Chura is not a lion, Chura only makes the croaking sound. replied the frog.

🐾 🐾 🐾 🐾

"yikes!!! nobody can teach me
how to roar like my papa", Simba
thought to himself.

"Oh no!!! I can not be like papa if I
can't roar like papa", he says
sadly as he begins to cry.
🐾 🐾 🐾 🐾

"Why do you cry my love?", Mama asks.

"Nobody in Mnyama kingdom can teach me how to roar like papa", says Simba.

"That's not true!!!", Mama surprisingly replies,

"I'm sure your papa will be happy to teach you, hurry along he is resting under the tree," says mama.

🐾 🐾 🐾 🐾

"Papa!!! can you please teach me how to roar? ", Simba asks.

"Ah! ah! my dear, you have the ability to roar, I don't need to teach you" papa replies.

"But my roar is very little," Simba says as he starts crying.

🐾 🐾 🐾 🐾

"oh no! Don't cry my dear," papa begs,
"I was once like you, it takes time, patience, and lots of practice for your little roar to grow thick and loud like mine.
Don't worry you will grow up to be a king just like me," says Papa.

"Thanks, Papa!" Simba says happily.

"Hey Simba, can you now roar like your Papa," his friends ask.
"Not yet, my roar is still little, papa said that my roar will be as loud as his when I grow up," Simba replies.
"When will you grow up?" his friends ask.
"Papa said it takes time and patience for young ones like us to grow up. Simba replies.

🐾 🐾 🐾 🐾

THE END

ROAR!

HELLO

www.ingramcontent.com/pod-product-compliance
Lightning Source LLC
Chambersburg PA
CBHW041552040426
42447CB00002B/151